First World War
and Army of Occupation
War Diary
France, Belgium and Germany

25 DIVISION
75 Infantry Brigade,
Brigade Trench Mortar Battery
21 March 1916 - 31 May 1916

WO95/2251/6

The Naval & Military Press Ltd
www.nmarchive.com
Published in association with The National Archives

Published by

The Naval & Military Press Ltd

Unit 10 Ridgewood Industrial Park,

Uckfield, East Sussex,

TN22 5QE England

Tel: +44 (0) 1825 749494

www.naval-military-press.com

www.nmarchive.com

This diary has been reprinted in facsimile from the original. Any imperfections are inevitably reproduced and the quality may fall short of modern type and cartographic standards.

© **Crown Copyright**
Images reproduced by permission of The National Archives, London, England, 2015.

Contents

Document type	Place/Title	Date From	Date To
Heading	WO95/2251-6		
Heading	75th Trench Mortar Bty Mar 1916 To May 1916		
Heading	75/2 Trench Mortar Battery, May 1916		
War Diary	Candas	21/03/1916	22/03/1916
War Diary	Bryas	23/03/1916	28/03/1916
War Diary	Bailleol-Aux-Cornailles	29/03/1916	31/03/1916
War Diary	Candas	21/03/1916	22/03/1916
War Diary	Bryas	23/03/1916	28/03/1916
War Diary	Bailleul-Ause Cornailles	29/03/1916	31/03/1916
War Diary	Ligny St Flochel	29/04/1916	29/04/1916
War Diary	Newerth St Vaast	30/04/1916	31/05/1916

bo 95/2251/6.

25TH DIVISION
75TH INFY BDE

75TH TRENCH MORTAR BTY
MAR 1916 to MAY 1916

75th Inf. Bde.

25th Division

75/2 TRENCH MORTAR BATTERY,

MAY, 1916.

(Battery formed 29.4.16).

75/1 TRENCH MORTAR BATTERY.

WAR DIARY / INTELLIGENCE SUMMARY

Army Form C. 2118.

Place	Date	Hour	Summary of Events and Information	Remarks and references to Appendices
CANDAS	2/3/16	4 P.M.	Battery formed at 3rd Army School of Mortars. Personnel & guns complete, but men's equipment very deficient. Guns are 4 - 3" Stokes Mortars.	
"	22/3/16	4 P.M.	Left School of Mortars, proceeding by train from CANDAS to ST POL, thence by road to 75th INF. BDE.	
		7 P.M.	Arr. at 75th INF BDE. at BRYAS.	
BRYAS			Kit inspection, & indents put in for deficiencies.	
"	23/3/16	9.30 A.M. / 2.30 P.M.	Training (Squad drill, without rifles, & gun drill)	
"	24/3/16	ditto	ditto	
"	25/3/16	ditto	"	Payment of battery 25/3/16 est. 1/-
"	26/3/16	10.30 A.M.	Inspection of battery & marching order & of gun by G.O.C. 75th INF. BDE.	
"		11.30 A.M.	Lecture by O.C. battery on N.C.O.'s + men on emplacement & protection of trench mortars in the line.	
"	27/3/16	9.30 A.M. / 2.30 P.M.	Training (Squad drill, without rifles, & gun drill).	
"	28/3/16	9.30 A.M.	Marched with Brigade to BAILLEUL-AUX-CORNAILLES. Guns & kit sent in advance by lorry. 2/Lt.	
BAILLEUL-AUX-CORNAILLES	29/3/16	9.30 A.M. / 2.30 P.M.	Training (Squad drill, without rifles, & gun drill)	A.J. Newton joined T.M. Bn.
"	30/3/16	ditto	Inspection of Brigade & of battery at gun drill by G.O.C.	
"	31/3/16	11 A.M.		
"		2.30 P.M.	PAYMENT OF BATTERY.	Comdg. 75/1 1/4/16

75/1 TRENCH MORTAR BATTERY WAR DIARY

Place	Date	Hour	Summary of Events and Information	Remarks and reference to Appendices
Cardas	21/3/16	4 P.M.	Battery formed at 3rd Army School of Mortars. Personnel 3 guns complete, but men's equipment very deficient, guns are 4. 3" STOKES MORTARS	
"	22/3/16	4 A.M.	Left School of Mortars, proceeding by train to ST POL thence by lorry & bus to 75th INF BDE at BRYAS.	
Bryas	23/3/16	2 P.M.	Kit inspection & indents sent in for deficiencies	
"	23/3/16	9.30 AM to 12.30 PM	Training (Squad drill without rifles and gun drill)	
"	24/3/16	Ditto	Ditto	
"	25/3/16	Ditto	Ditto	
"	25/3/16	2 P.M.	Payment of Battery	
"	26/3/16	10.30 AM	Inspection of Battery in marching order & guns by L.O.C. 75th INF. BDE	
"	"	11.30 AM	Lecture by O.C. Battery to N.C.O.s & men on employment & protection of Trench Mortars in the line	
"	27/3/16	9.30 AM to 12.30 PM	Training (Squad drill without rifles & Gun Drill)	
"	28/3/16	9.30 AM	Marched with Brigade to Bailleul-Aux-Cornailles guns and kit went in advance by lorry	
Bailleul Aux Cornailles	29/3/16	9.30 AM to 12.30 PM	Training (Squad drill without rifles and gun drill)	
"	30/3/16	9.30 AM to 12.30 PM	Ditto	"
"	31/3/16	11 A.M.	Inspection of Brigade & of Battery at gun drill by L.O.C. on L.	
"	"	2 P.M.	Payment of Battery	

H. Wainforth ? Lt.
Commanding 75/1 T.M. BTY

Army Form C. 2118.

WAR DIARY
or
INTELLIGENCE SUMMARY

(Erase heading not required.)

75/2 Trench Mortar B?y

Place	Date	Hour	Summary of Events and Information	Remarks and references to Appendices
Lignereuil	29/4/16		Battery formed on conclusion of course at 3rd Army School of Mortars.	
Neuville St Vaast	30/4/16	9 a.m.	Proceeded to ECOIVRES. Took over right sector of trenches of 75th B?e from 75/1 B?y, 2nd and 8th Claws in occupation alternately.	
"	1/5/16		Repair work on emplacements. Continued in subsequent days.	
"	4/5/16	6.0 p.m.	Registered with two guns from LICHFIELD ST. and STAFFORD ST. 6 bombs (prepared by prior occupants) fails to explode.	
"	6.5.16	7.30 p.m.	Registered on head C.T. at A4 d 4.2.50? shells exploded.	
"	7.5.16		Ranging and construction of emplacements continued.	
"	8.5.16		Ditto	
"	9.5.16		Establishment of ammunition fired at 240, and drawn in accordance.	
"	10.5.16		Experimented with wooden frame for base plate of Stokes gun, made according to design at B?e shop. Force of recoil proved too strong for frame.	1
"	11.5.16	5.30 p.m.	Carried out with R.A. an offensive against enemy line Trench at A4 d 5.5 (Sheet 51 B – Roclincourt). Much material damage effected. No enemy retaliation.	
"	12.5.16	3.30 p.m.	Fired 8 rounds on M.G. emplacement at A4 d 3.6, 3.2 (Sheet 51 B). Unobserved.	
"	13.5.16		Quiet day.	
"	14.5.16		ditto	
"	15.5.16		Intermittent fire by Trotter German M.Gs.	
"	16.5.16	6.30 p.m.	Fired 57 shells on German CTs and Stokes tracks. Much material thrown up.	
"	17.5.16		5 rounds were fired into German wire working party. Repairing damage.	
"	18.5.16		Quiet day. Enemy fired rifle grenades.	
"	19.5.16		ditto	
"	20.5.16		ditto	
"	21.5.16		ditto	
"	22.5.16		Enemy T.M. little done by Batt?s line firing reduced to a minimum by B?e	
"	23.5.16		Fired 23 rounds into Silesian enemy	

WAR DIARY
INTELLIGENCE SUMMARY

Army Form C. 2118.

Place	Date	Hour	Summary of Events and Information	Remarks and references to Appendices
Mauser Silmont	27.5.16	2 noon	G.O.C Brigade inspected emplacements. Fired 20 rounds of average Mortar at 2nd line obtaining good low air bursts.	
	28.5.16		Quiet day. D mine was let off at 1 a.m. effort of 176 Redoubt (to front of Sept Div.)	
	29.5.16	6 p.m.	Operation reported. Trench Mortars of Ayd 3,7,5 (576 Redoubt). 60 rounds fired with F.W. effect. (XVII Corps Int. Summary No 101 reports "Our strikes were in conjunction with Eighteen Carried out an effective bombardment. Enemy front line and C.T.S. doing a good deal of damage.")	
	29.5.16		Gordons retaliated with heavy rifle fire on our defence line.	
	30.5.16	10.30 p.m.	Operation with howitzers and other artillery on Ayd 4, 3.5 and other targets (51E). Trench Mortars and artillery bombarded (Ayd 1-5, No 103 21/15/16 Say. Own trenches were reported doing a good deal of damage. The enemy trenches about Ayd 4, 3 showing a good deal of damage.	
	31.5.16	9 p.m.	2nd S. Lanc's relieved by 1/5 Gordon Highlanders (1 Coy) and 1/6 Black Watch (2 platoons)	

Oscar Lloyd Lieut.

O.C. 75/2 D.M. Bty.

www.ingramcontent.com/pod-product-compliance
Lightning Source LLC
Chambersburg PA
CBHW081253170426
43191CB00037B/2147